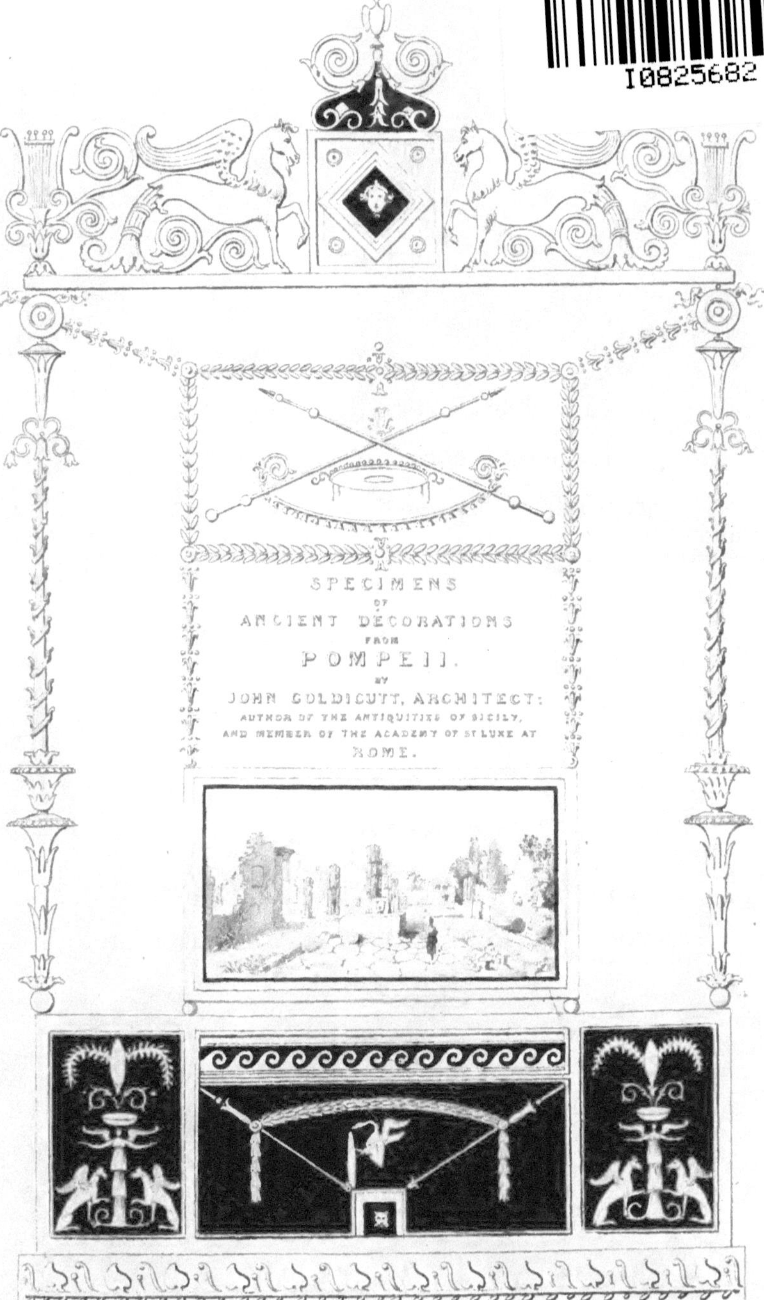

Drawn by John Goldicutt.

Engraved by Edwd Finden.

British Library Cataloguing-in-Publication Data
A catalogue record for this book is available from the
British Library

A Short Introduction to the History of Pompeii

Pompeii was an ancient Roman town-city near the modern Italian city of Naples. It is famed for being one of the ill-feted settlements destroyed and buried by the massive eruption of Mount Vesuvius in 79 AD. Along with Herculaneum, Pompeii is of particular interest and historical importance due to its preservation under the several metres of volcanic ash and pumice, protecting it from air and moisture. This created a snapshot of a moment in an ancient civilisation that would otherwise have been eroded by time.

It is believed to have been founded by Osci in the sixth or seventh century BC. By the 4th century it was under the control of the Roman Empire, finally being conquered and becoming a Roman colony in 80 BC following an unsuccessful rebellion against the Republic. At the time of its destruction, Pompeii had a population of around 11,000 and a well developed infrastructure comprising a port, an amphitheatre, a gymnasium, and a complex water system.

The first evidence of the demise of this settlement came in the form of a letter written by Pliny the Younger, the Roman, lawyer, author, and magistrate. In the letter he describes the death of his uncle, Pliny the Elder, an admiral of the Roman fleet, and his demise while trying to rescue the citizens of Pompeii. However, it was not until 1599, when a channel was being dug to divert the river Samo, that the entombed settlement was re-discovered. Domenica Fonatana, a Swiss architect, was called in for his opinion on the finding. He uncovered several frescoes but then decided to cover them over again. Nobody knows exactly why he did this – some see it as a forward-thinking act of preservation, while others contend that the sexual content of many of the works may not have been considered 'good taste' during the counter-reformation period.

If it was an act of censorship then he was certainly not alone in his opinion. When King Francis of Naples visited the Pompeii exhibition at the national Gallery in 1819, he was so embarrassed at being exposed to the artwork, while in the company of his wife and daughter, that he ordered some of it to be locked away in a secret cabinet for the eyes of "people of mature age and respected morals" only. After being opened and closed again several times over the next two hundred years the exhibit reopened in 2000, but it is still not allowed to be viewed by minors unless in the presence of a guardian or with written permission. Aside from the art of the lost city, many other aspects of ancient life were also preserved, such as clothes, coins, furniture, food, and the bodies of the unfortunate residents. Previously it was thought that they had been killed by ash suffocation, but recent testing indicates that they died an instant death from the searing heat of the eruption.

Pompeii is now a hugely popular tourist destination and a UNESCO heritage site. Since the town's excavation however, its exposure to the elements has led to much erosion and many of the buildings are in dire need of restoration. Conservation of such a site is both time consuming and expensive, and an estimated $335 million is needed for the necessary repair work. Pompeii provides us with a fascinating window into the daily lives of an ancient civilisation though, and with one third of the city still to be uncovered, is likely to continue presenting us with yet more insights into a culture frozen in time.

The following Designs from Pompeii (or, as it is called by the Italians, Pompeja) were made with a view to assist the Artist in the interior decoration of houses, as well in what regards figure as colour. It was formerly a general notion, that the same species of Architecture which was used on the outside of houses was as applicable to the inside of them, and hence the same heavy forms, the massy column, and cumbrous architrave and pediment, &c. were adopted in rooms as in porticos, though the same reasons for their use did not exist, and the difference of distances and lights under which these things were seen, rendered what was becoming in the one case, ridiculous in the other. The discovery of an ancient town, however, as Walpole justly remarks, shows that the Ancients had not committed the blunder which we thought we were imitating, and opened to us the view of a more festive and imaginative species of decoration. Their arrangements of colour appear to have been as happy as their combination of forms, and may, I think, be as useful to the Artist or Amateur who may study them.

The Plates of the present, as well as those of the following numbers, represent generally the elevation of the side of an apartment. To describe them separately as to precise locality may not be necessary; it is sufficient that they are, with little exception, a perfect imitation of the original, both in form and colour.

There are two specimens of ceilings from a portion of the remains, called Marcus Arrius Diomede's Villa.

The Mosaic pavement is from the same interesting source.

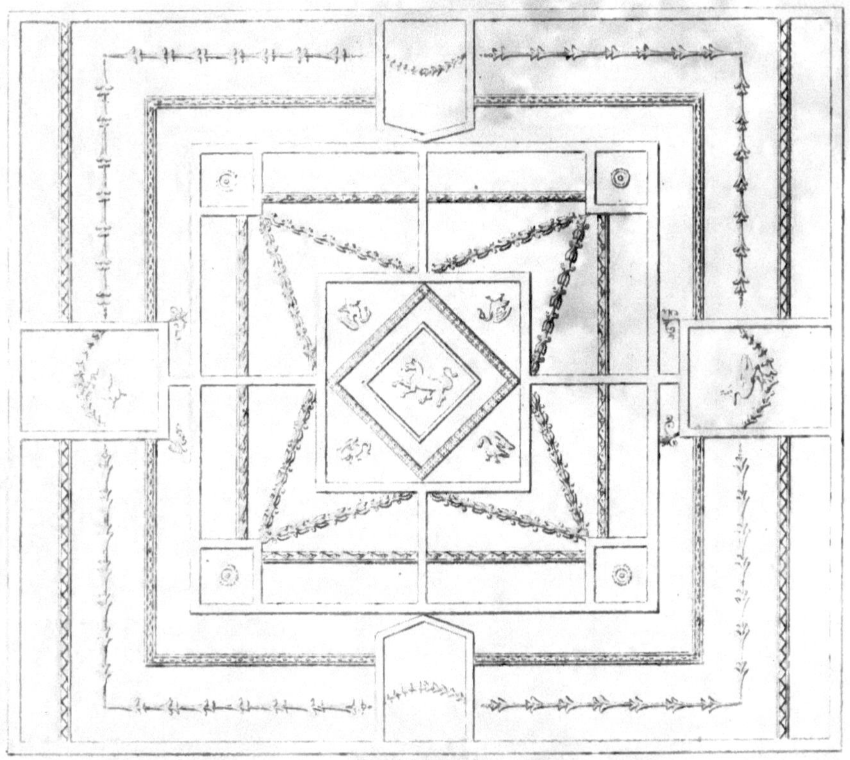

Drawn by John Goldicutt.

CEILING.

London, Published April 1820, by Rodwell & Martin, New Bond Street.

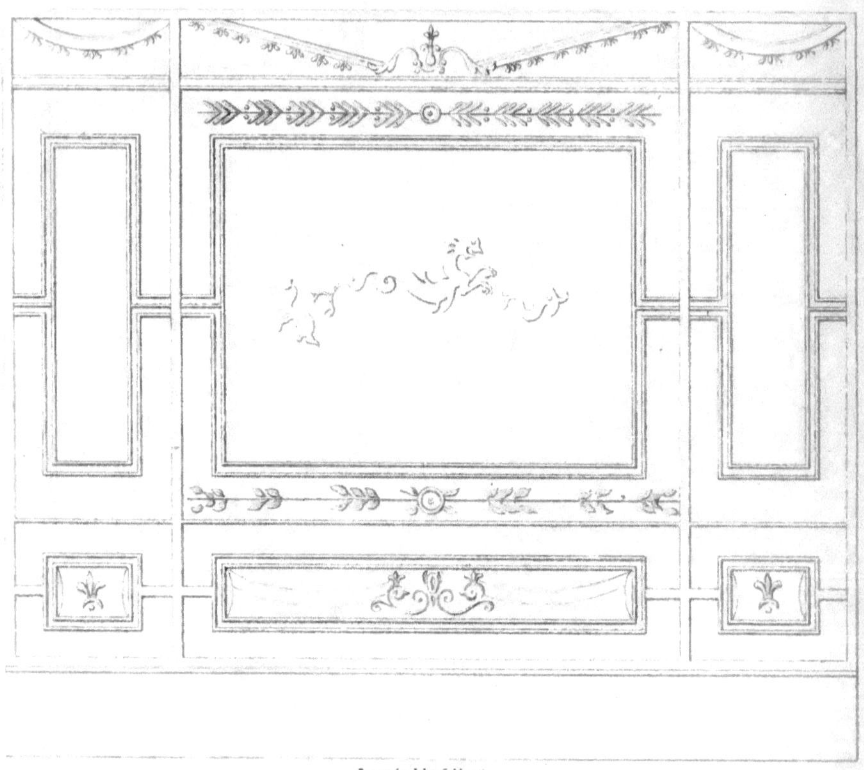

Drawn by John Goldicutt

SIDE OF AN APARTMENT.

London. Published April 1825, by Rodwell & Martin, New Bond Street

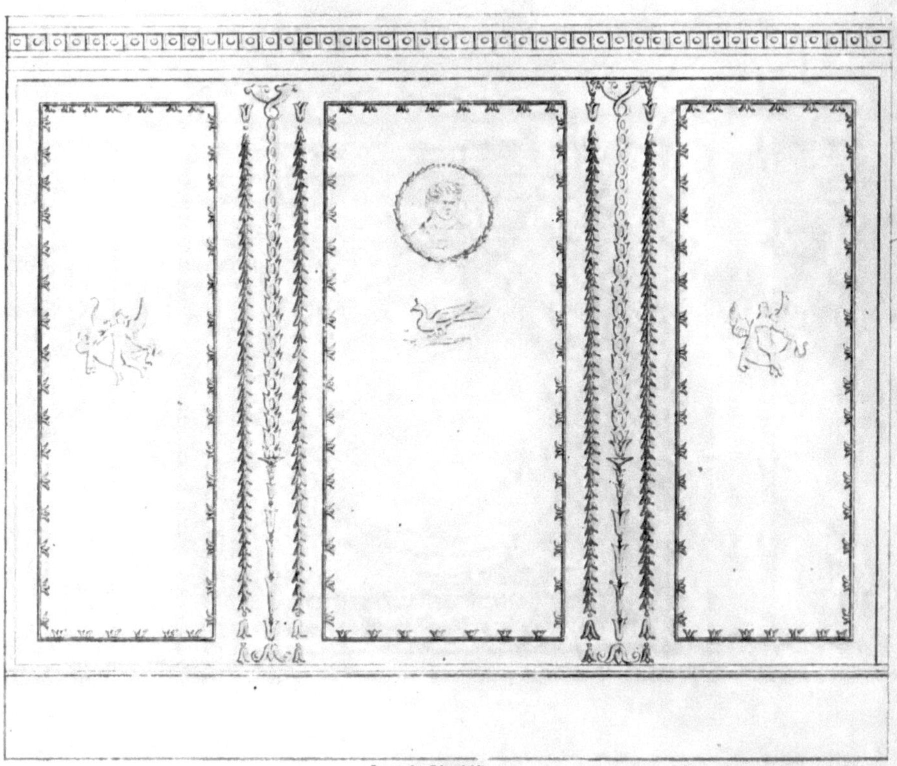

Drawn by John Goldicutt.

SIDE OF AN APARTMENT.

London, Published April 1825, by Rodwell & Martin, New Bond Street

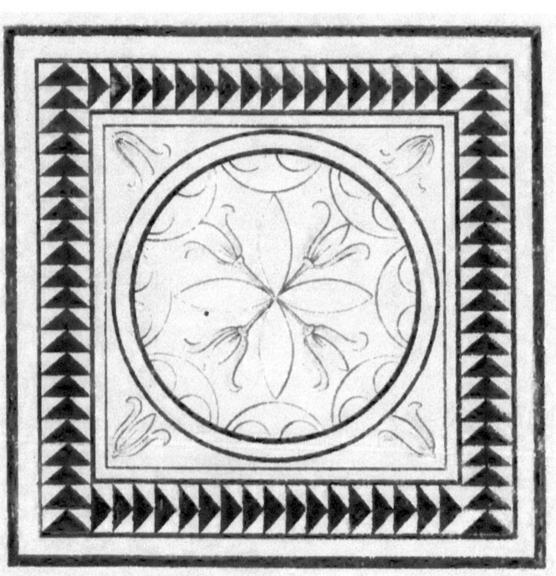

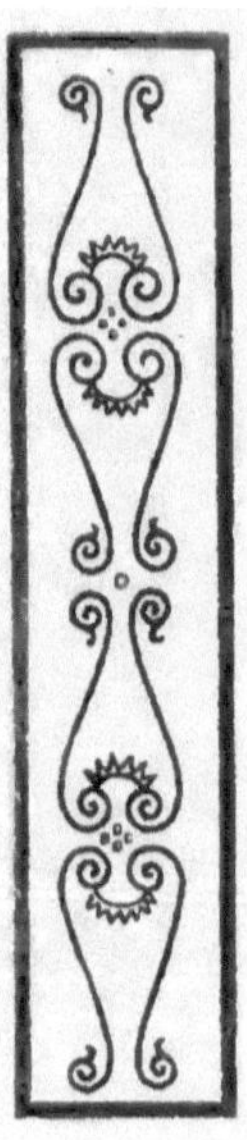

Drawn by John Goldicutt.

MOSAIC PAVEMENT.

London, Published April 1825, by Rodwell & Martin, New Bond Street.

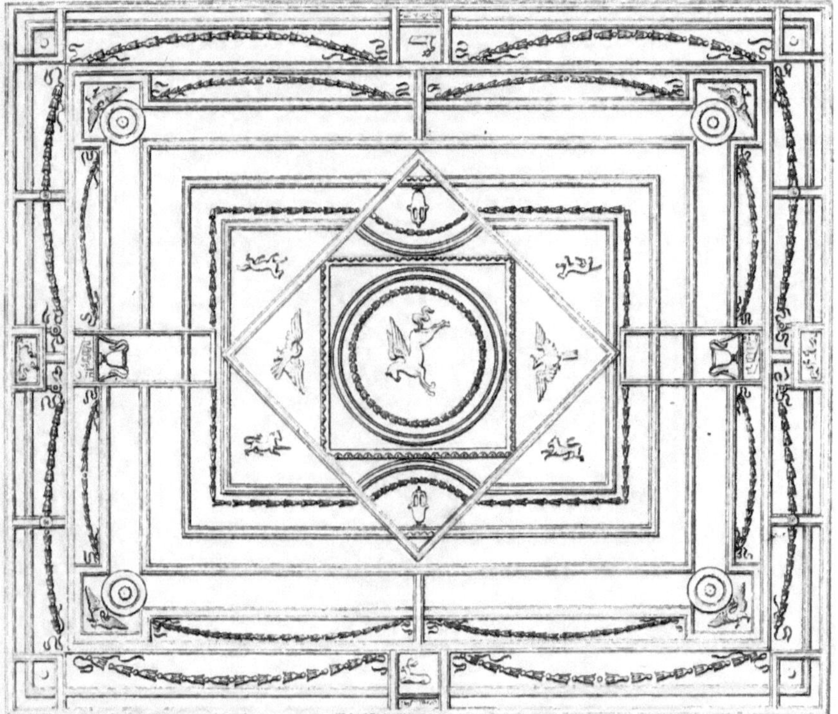

Drawn by John Goldicutt.

CEILING.

London, Published June 1828, by Rodwell & Martin, New Bond Street.

Drawn by John Goldicutt.

SIDE OF AN APARTMENT.

London. Published June 1825, by Rodwell & Martin, New Bond Street.

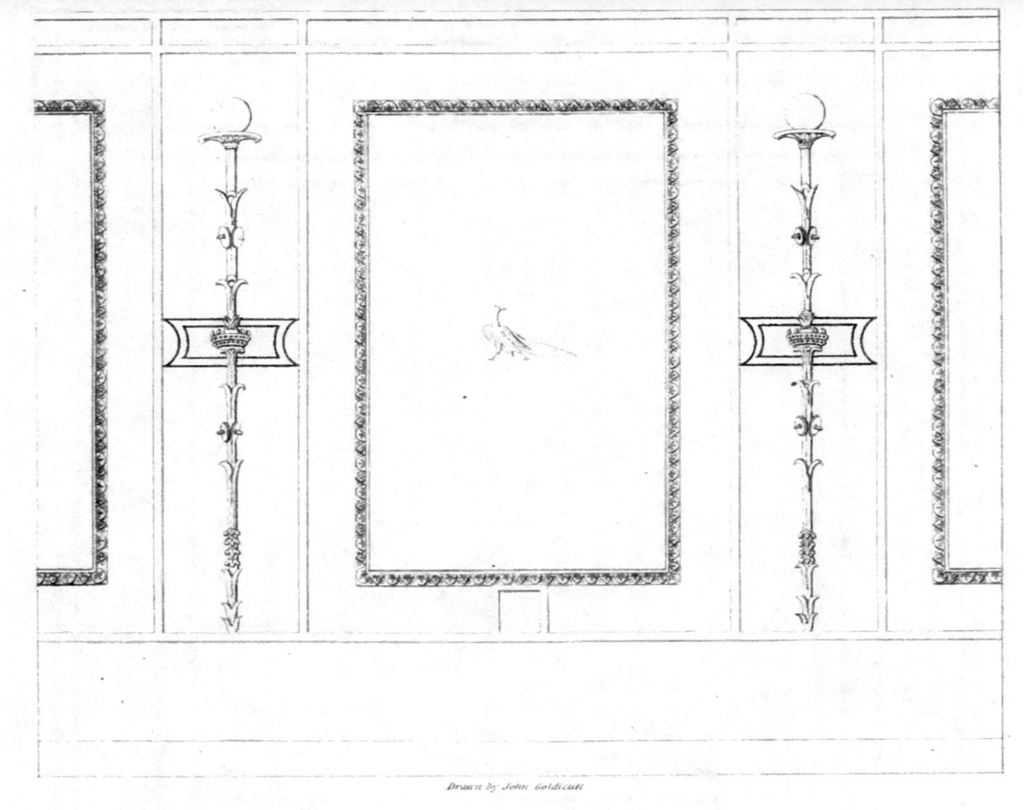

Drawn by John Goldicutt

SIDE OF AN APARTMENT.

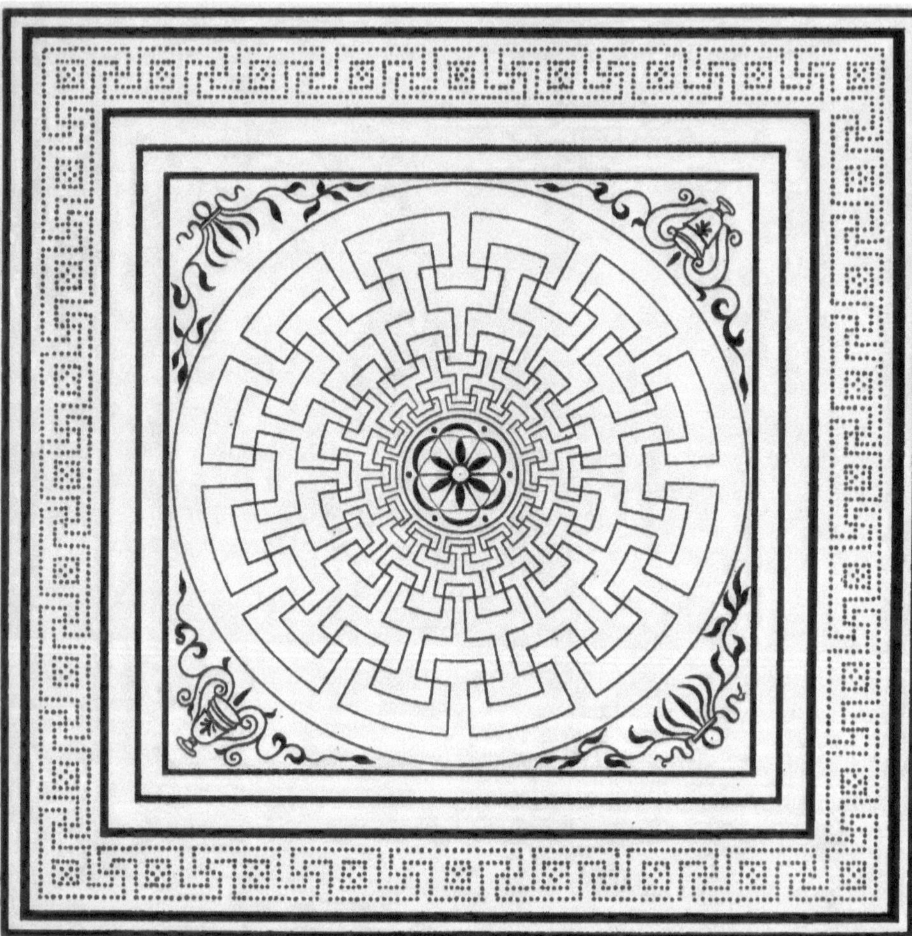

Drawn by John Goldicutt.

MOSAIC PAVEMENT.

London. Published June 1825, by Rodwell & Martin. New Bond Street

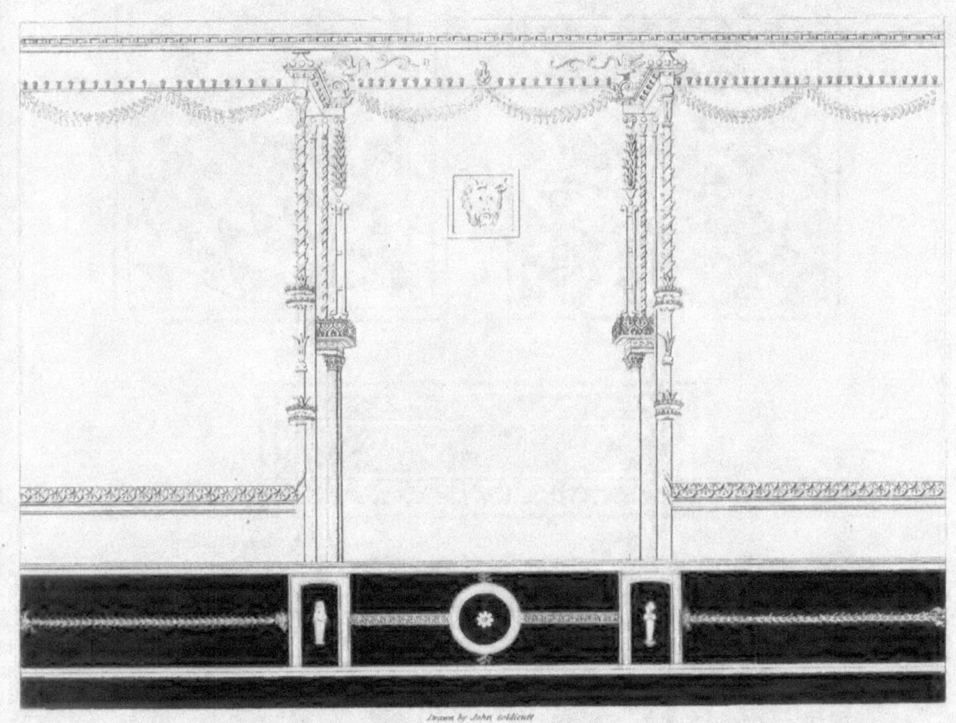

Drawn by John Goldicutt

SIDE OF AN APARTMENT

London. Published June 1825, by Rodwell & Martin, New Bond Street.

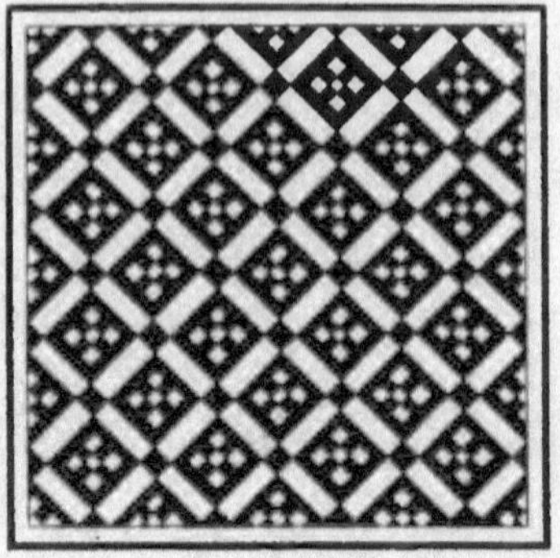

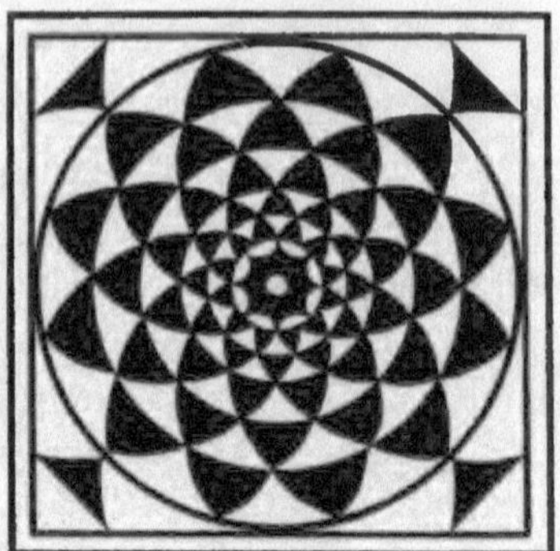

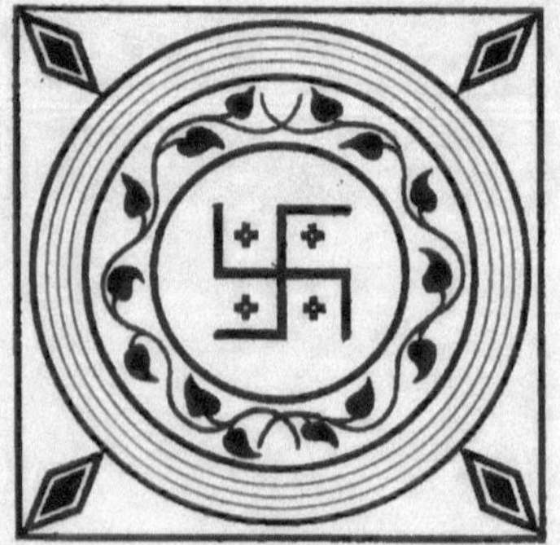

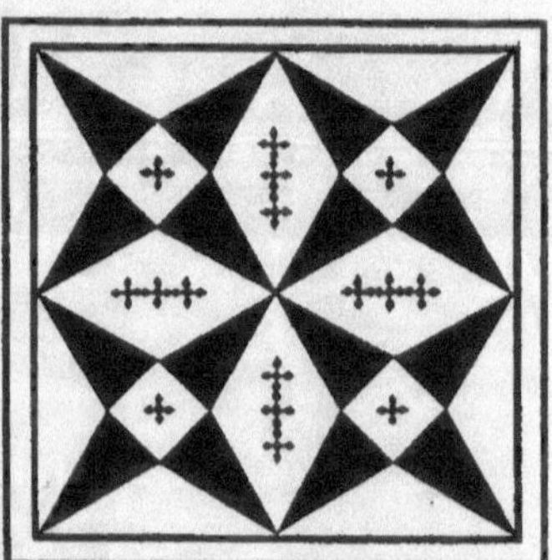

Drawn by John Goldicutt.

MOSAIC PAVEMENT.

London, Published 1825, by Rodwell & Martin, New Bond Street

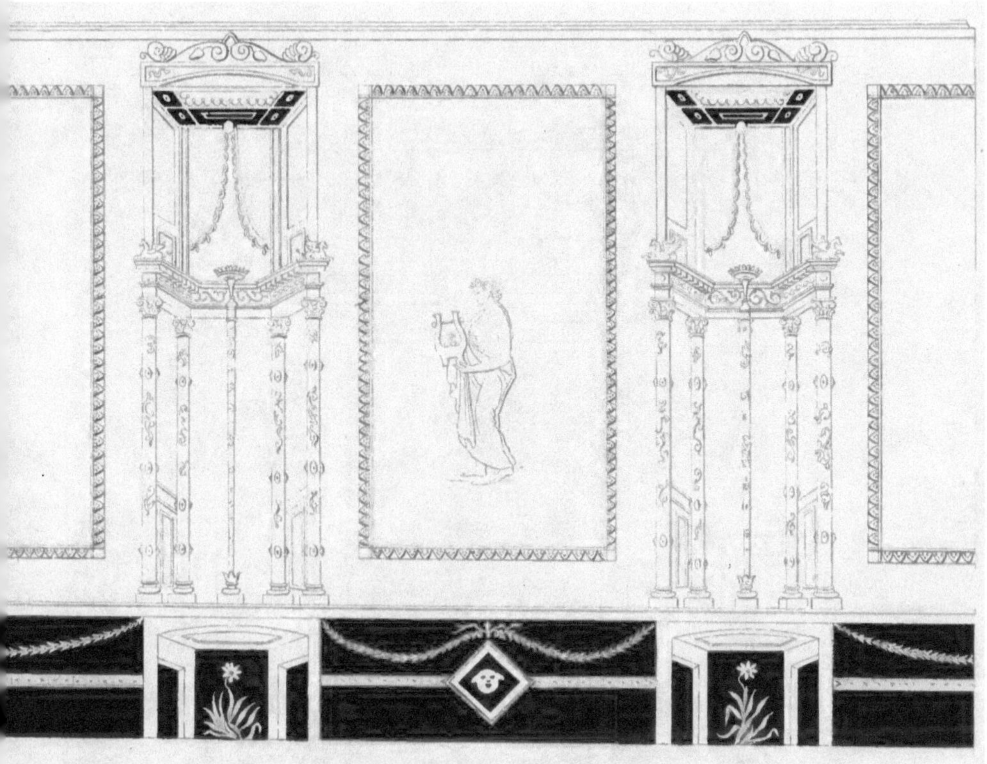

Drawn by John Goldicutt

SIDE OF AN APARTMENT.

London, Published 1825, by Rodwell & Martin New Bond Street.

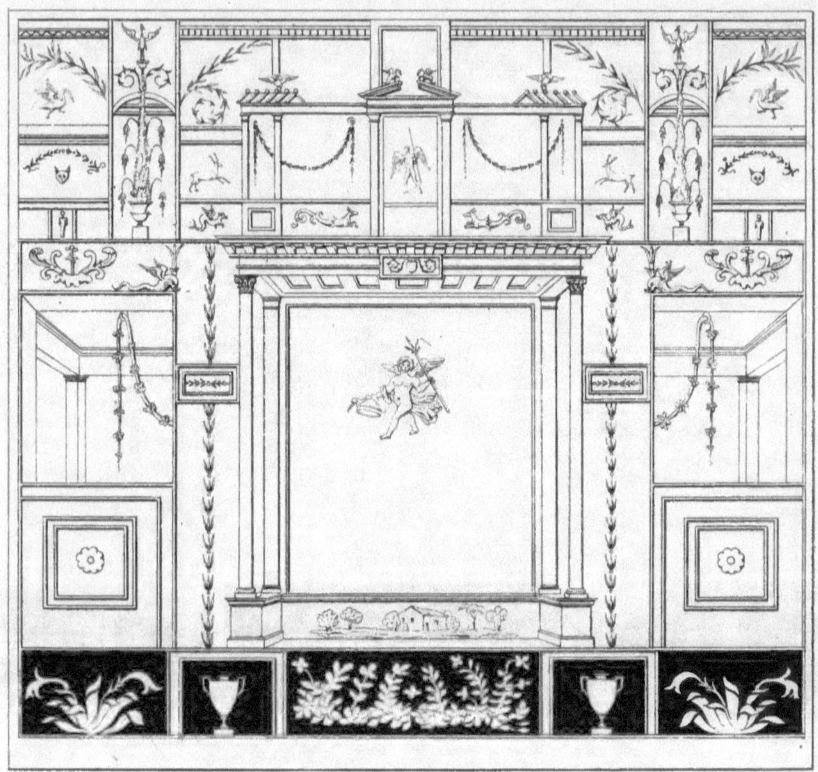

Drawn by John Goldicutt.

SIDE OF AN APARTMENT.

London, Published 1825, by Rodwell & Martin, New Bond Street.

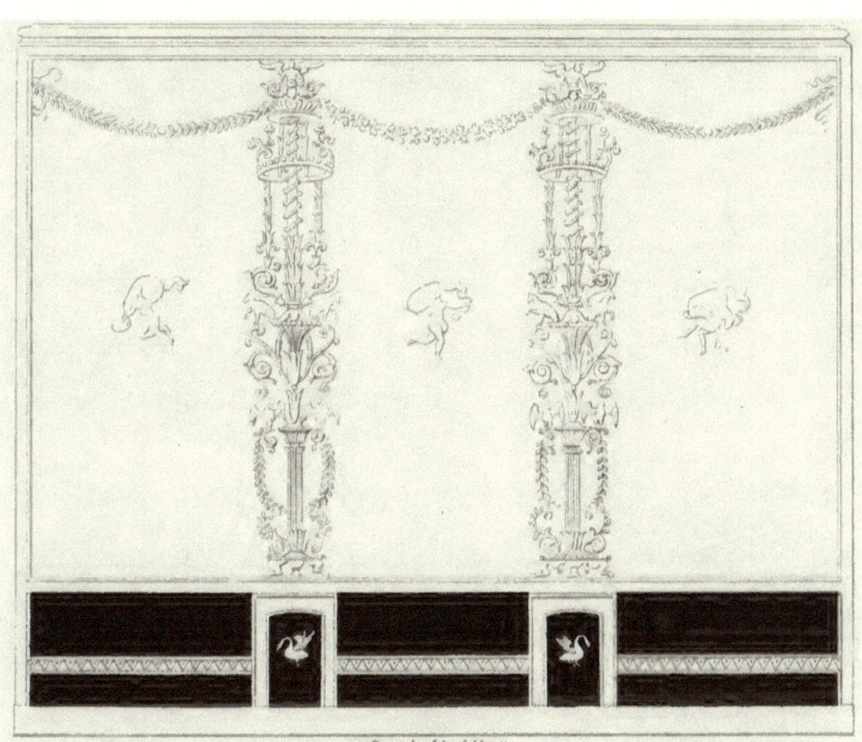

Drawn by John Goldicutt.

SIDE OF AN APARTMENT.

London, Published 1825, by Rodwell & Martin, New Bond Street

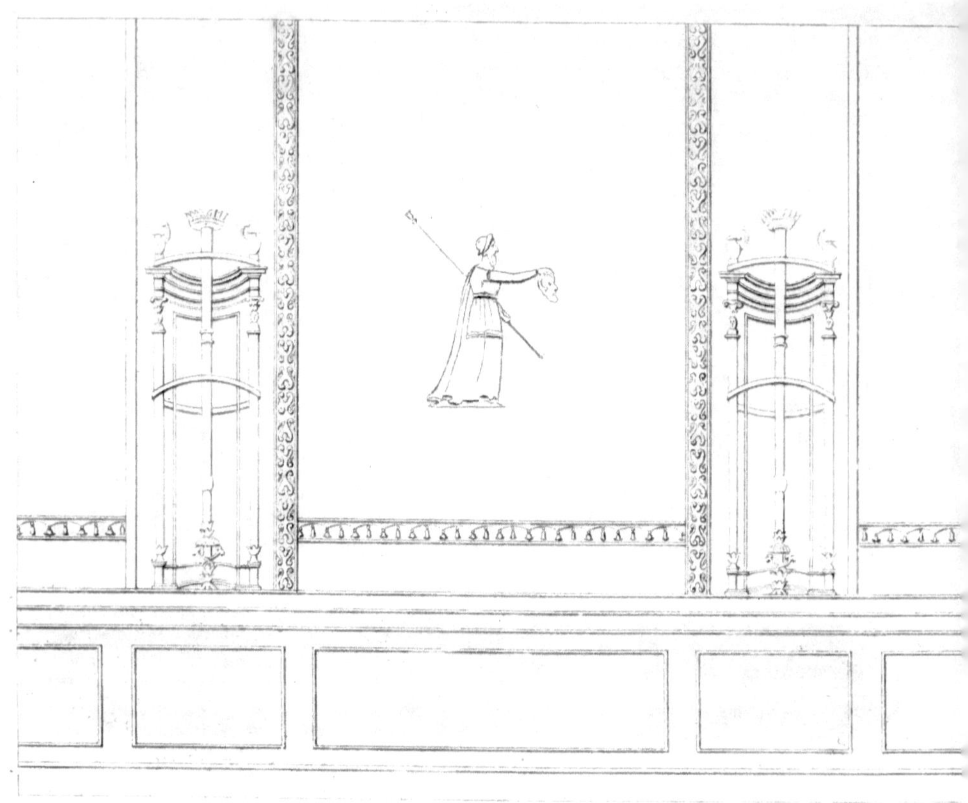

Drawn by John Goldicutt, from a Sketch by A. Poynter, Architect

SIDE OF AN APARTMENT.

London, Published 1825, by Rodwell & Martin, New Bond Street.

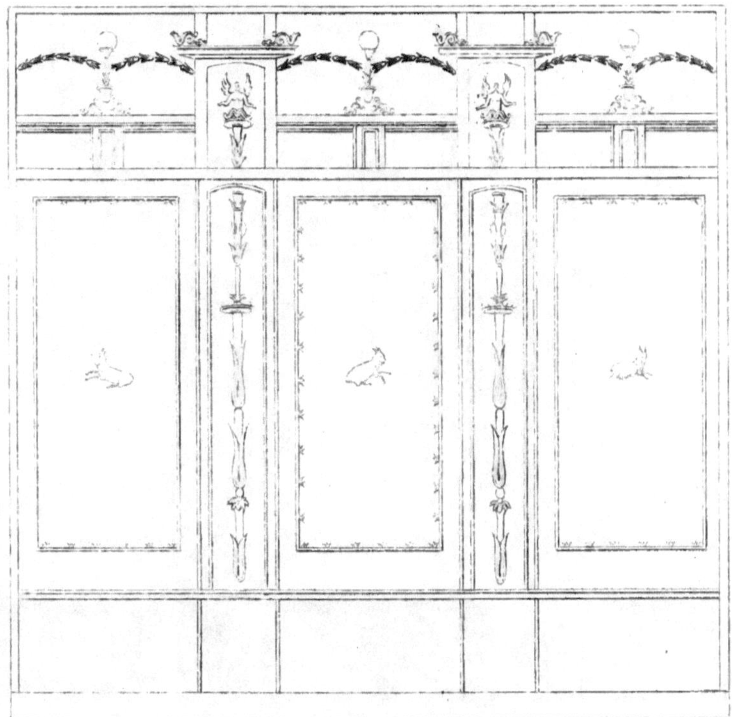

Drawn by John Goldicutt.

SIDE OF AN APARTMENT.

London, Published 1825, by Rodwell & Martin, New Bond Street.

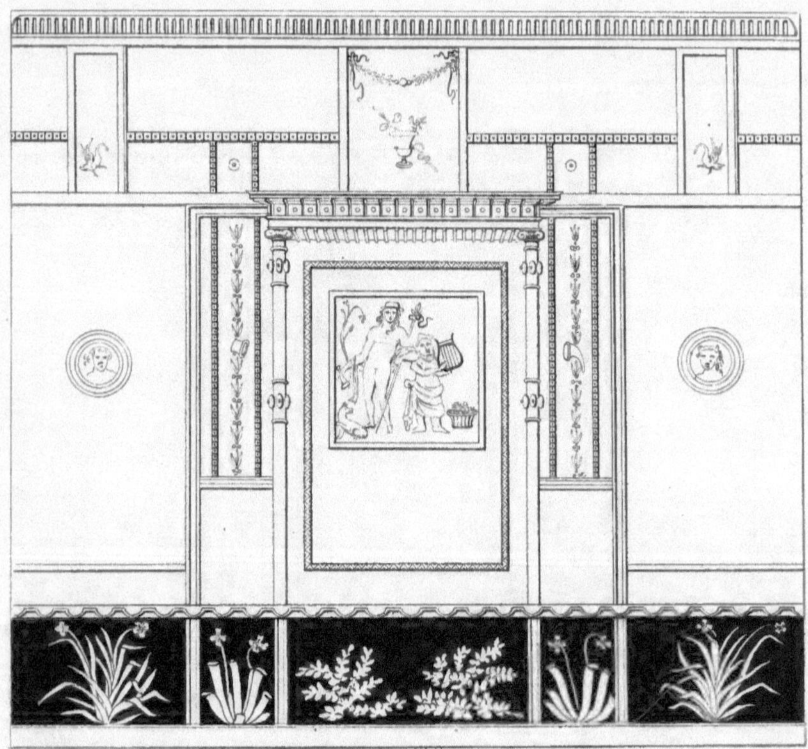

Drawn by John Goldicutt.

SIDE OF AN APARTMENT.

London, Published 1825, by Rodwell & Martin, New Bond Street

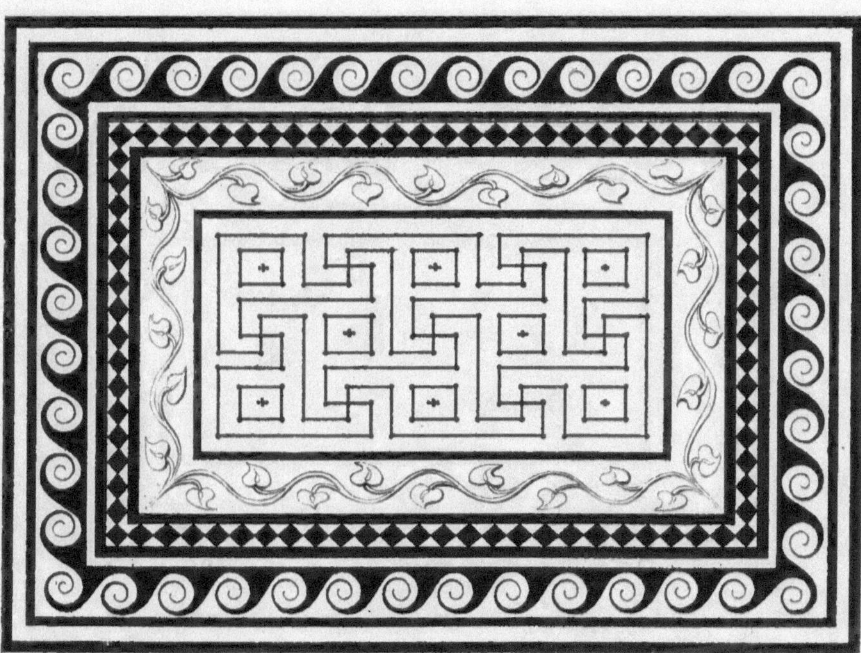

Drawn by John Goldicutt.

MOSAIC PAVEMENT.

London, Published 1825 by Rodwell & Martin, New Bond Street

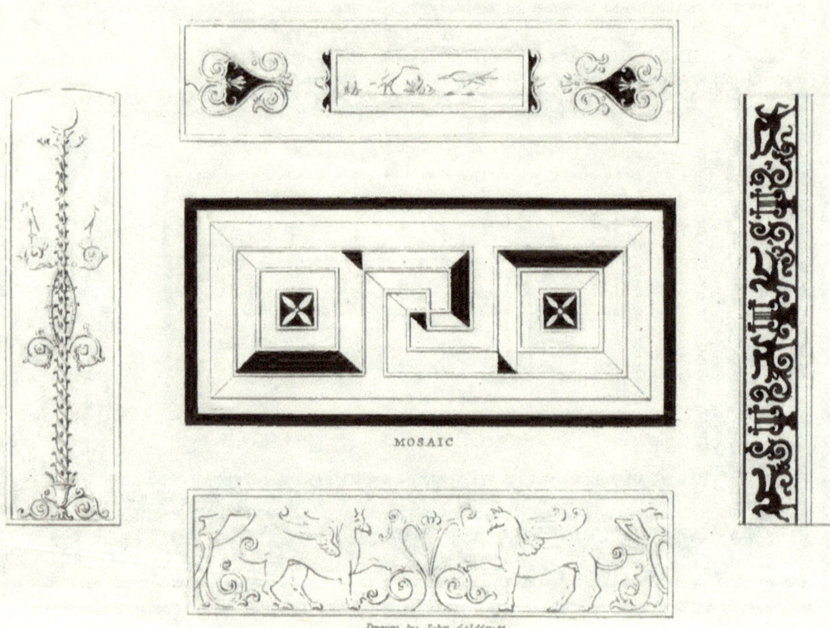

Drawn by John Goldicutt.

FRAGMENTS.

London. Published 1825, by Rodwell & Martin, New Bond Street

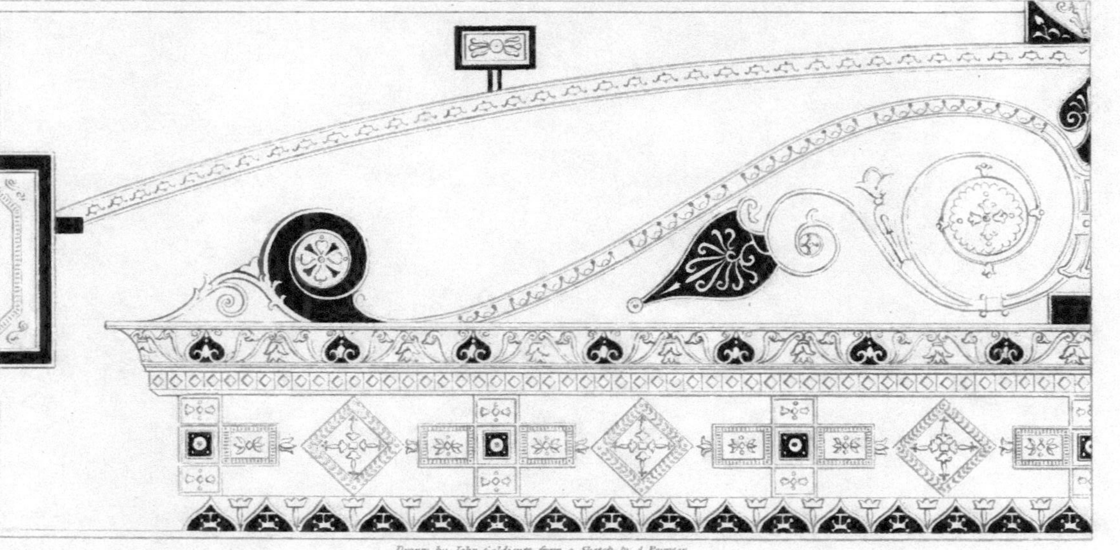

Drawn by John Goldicutt, from a Sketch by A. Poynter

A FRAGMENT.

London, Published 1825, by Rodwell & Martin, New Bond Street

www.ingramcontent.com/pod-product-compliance
Lightning Source LLC
LaVergne TN
LVHW041929090826
845145LV00017B/2782

* 9 7 8 1 4 7 3 3 2 1 8 2 3 *